START-UPS INNOVATION

FAST LANE

By Alistair J. Schneider

Email: alistair@startupsinnovation.com

Alistair J. Schneider, Publisher / Editorial Director

Yvonne Rose/Quality Press, Production Coordinator

legal advice or other expert assistance is required, the services of a competent professional person should be sought.

EBooks are available at special discounts for bulk purchases, sales promotions, fund raising or educational purposes.

"You have to learn the rules of the game. And then you have to play better than anyone else."

- Albert Einstein

CONTENTS

Foreword by Bernard Kress   5

About   7

Author's introduction   7

The author's motivations for writing this e-book: 9

Who should read this book?   10

Let's get started   11

First, what is a start-up?   11

Attitudes of successful entrepreneurs   13

The Attitudes of successful entrepreneurs   13

Start-ups, innovation friendly environments and key players   17

Defining your start-up idea   23

What is your business idea?   23

Conduct your market research   28

Completing a pitch presentation and executive summary   31

The traditional Pitch presentation slides: 32

Executive Summary   34

The 60-seconds pitch presentation: 35

Gain traction early   36

Create your online presence   37

Networking   38

Test your market traction   41

Fund your idea and start-up!   44

   Financing choices   44

   Crowdfunding in a nutshell   46

   Get funded by "accredited investors"   48

      Investors criteria (SEC Rule)   48

      Key steps & tips   49

         Understanding what investors usually look for.   49

         Connecting with investors   51

         Pitching your idea clearly & concisely to the investor(s) 51

         Investor's further due diligence   53

         Funding rounds   53

      Legal aspects to start-up   54

         Consult with a lawyer   55

         Delaware C-Corporation   55

         Stock Purchase agreements   55

         Employment agreements   56

         Employee Stock Options   56

         Non-disclosure agreement   56

         Intellectual property   56

Conclusion   57

About the Author: Alistair Schneider   59

Author's Acknowledgements: 62

Bernard Kress, resident of Silicon Valley, serial entrepreneur and Executive at Microsoft, with a background in optical engineering with emphasis on micro-optics and holographic technologies, applied to Virtual reality (VR), Augmented Reality (AR) and Smart glasses products. Bernard is also a professor at University, instructor of short courses, international conference chair, speaker (UNESCO), and author of numerous books on this technology (published by John Wiley and Sons, McGraw Hill). Throughout two decades spent in the Silicon Valley, he has launched numerous start-ups, helped develop several industrial and consumer products, and holds more than 30 international patents. He has worked lately with some of the most innovative companies in the world to develop some of the most exciting consumer products, such as Glass at Google [X] Labs and HoloLens at Microsoft.

<u>Here is his message to you</u>:

Having been a serial entrepreneur and engineer working on new product or start-up launches throughout my career I have learned that innovation for the sake of innovation is not enough. You need to have the right idea, at the right time with the right people, developing the right technology that is solving a problem for an existing market. While it is absolutely crucial to master your field, it is as important to have a deep understanding of your competitive landscape and to surround yourself with complementary people that are in the right mindset and environment. Being innovative or saying you want to be innovative doesn't mean you will be successful. Launching a start-up is not an easy task, but it is possible. Especially, in the era in which we are now, where more tools and information are available to everyone. Alistair, the author of this e-book, provides the reader with a very thorough overview of the start-up process for early-stage entrepreneurs, what one should expect through the different stages of the start-up development, the good as well as the bad. He shows how the entrepreneur should prepare him/herself in order to anticipate various early-stage hurdles rather than experience them, and thus have the best chances of making the best impact. This is done in a simple, concise and methodic way. Apply Alistair's teachings to get the most out of your early-stage entrepreneurial experience and magnify your chances of success - a good place to start before you incorporate your company.

My personal message to readers is two-fold: First, you will learn as much from your mistakes as you will learn from your successes. Both are equally important for the early-stage entrepreneur. Secondly, never give up; even after a few successive failures, your knowledge and experience will only grow and make you a better fit for the implementation of your next big idea.

AUTHOR'S INTRODUCTION

What takes the most time to launch an idea is finding one that meets the market needs, having the right people around you, funds, and being in the right mentality. This e-book will equip you with some fundamentals of entrepreneurship (and intrapreneurship) that will help you understand what you need to accelerate your project's success. To write this e-book, I immersed myself in start-up eco-systems from the East to the West coast of the United States and observed ones from other regions of the world. I had discussions with key players and then synthesized some of the results of this experience. This is a first edition and will be improved, based on feedback. (Make sure to contact me at alistair@startupsinnovation.com)

As the world economic forum in January 2016 predicted the 4th industrial revolution, it has become easier every day for entrepreneurs to launch start-ups. Other authors close to the topic predict that we have entered the era of endless innovation. What this means is major opportunities and disruptions, as well as additional competitive pressure.

For entrepreneurs, it is an amazing time: new incubators, mentors, knowledge, resources, online communities, investors, and technologies are available to help them pursue limitless opportunities and work on the things they love and believe in. Crowdsourcing and crowdfunding sites are making it much easier to build a complementary team and get funding. In addition, many up-to-date governments, all around the world are now betting on start-ups to safeguard or grow their economies, placing in many cases the entrepreneur as a savior. They understand that if they don't rapidly create the incentives and infrastructure for start-ups and innovation they will experience or continue to see economic downturn, better products being developed in other regions of the world, or produced at lower costs in emerging regions, slower job creation or destruction and all the further problems that comes with these negative signs.

Yes! The rules of the game have changed: <u>We are in the innovation fast lane</u>. Many barriers to entry have fallen! This new era will belong to those who think like entrepreneurs, focus, and understand how to drive innovation. Steve Jobs once said "Innovation distinguishes between a leader and a follower" – exactly!

In response, you may have already noticed that more established businesses, major corporations and even traditional consulting firms adopt leaner tools and methods used by start-up entrepreneurs in order to accelerate innovation, change a company's culture and to better adapt to these more rapidly turning markets. Having a majority of regular 9-5 employees that are internally focused solely on their tasks is no longer sufficient to stay ahead of the curve, nor for a business to compete with now more and more savvy, nimble and agile start-up teams. An existing product can now be wiped off the map overnight!

This e-book aims to provide entrepreneurs and intrapreneurs with the steps, as used in key ecosystems, to launch a start-up project. As mentioned earlier, launching a new idea is much easier than it was a few decades ago. Still it can be a daunting process, especially for first timers, and failure rates are still relatively high. This e-book has been written to make the process hopefully clearer to you and to augment your chances of success.

THE AUTHOR'S MOTIVATIONS FOR WRITING THIS E-BOOK:

- **Purpose:** Innovation brings people together to work on problematics that benefit all or many.
- **Empower** great entrepreneurial minds that may not have had access yet to this type of information.
- **To contribute** to the acceleration of innovation in general and help entrepreneurs succeed in their enterprises.

This is the first version of this e-book. Based on feedback and suggestions, it will be improved.

Contact: alistair@startupsinnovation.com

WHO SHOULD READ THIS BOOK?

There are different categories of audience for this e-book. While they may be different in nature, these audiences have one thing in common. They all share our mission of bringing change in the world and in their industry of choice. This manual should serve the following groups and more:

- **Aspiring Start-up entrepreneurs, engineers or scientists** who want to jump the learning curve and launch their ideas.
- **Corporate Employees (Intrapreneurs)**, who may want to understand the start-up process in order to create a culture of entrepreneurship and maybe lean some of the processes.
- **Incubators, accelerators, Plug n' Play, Universities and Institutions** that want to provide their members with an extensive and easy-to-read manual to facilitate the innovative process.
- **Creatives and artists** can benefit a lot of using similar methods used by start-up to launch their artistic ventures. Especially in these hyper-competitive and crowded times. (The music consumption has never been as high while revenue has never been as low). In addition, they are many untapped opportunities for artists and creatives who are open to partner with start-ups or companies.

Before you start, let us get on the same page. We will begin by defining some key terms and establish an understanding of the start-up environment. The following are the three areas that we will cover:

- Defining what a start-up is
- Attitudes of a successful entrepreneur
- Characteristics of a good start-up environment: The Silicon Valley Case

FIRST, WHAT IS A START-UP?

Start-ups are extraordinary innovative projects that aim to resolve complex problems with the goal of achieving fast growth and market disruption by delivering a new solution that fulfils a clear market need.

Key characteristics of a start-up:

- A solution that responds clearly to the needs of many
- Or a powerful niche
- A business model designed for fast growth
- Product perceived to be 10X Better
- Expected return on investment of 10X or more
- Generally funded by Investors (Business angels, Venture Capital or own funds)

- The product is a highly innovative solution to a complex problem
- The team is generally made of highly skilled and expert individuals
- The team needs to be made of people able to deliver results
- High risk: It is said that 9 out 10 start-ups fail to succeed.

Note: The known reasons for these failures happen to be: the team, egos, the business model design and execution. As you launch your business idea, keep these in mind and mitigate these risks.

It is important to separate a normal business from a start-up business. A normal business will not usually provide the same return on investment and will not deliver the same fast growth and does not generally involve the same level of risk.

Start-up story: Google is a perfect example of a successful start-up. Larry Page and Sergey Brin founded Google in 1997 from a garage. Only a couple of years later, in June 1999, the Venture Capitalist Firms Sequoia Capital and Kleiner Perkins funded Google for 25 million dollars. Approximately 15 years later, 2015 Google's revenue is roughly 70 billion dollars and its market capitalization is valued at about 500 billion dollars. What started on the basis of its search engine Google has grown into a major corporation and one of the most innovative in the world. To this day, Google still strives to maintain a start-up mentality within its walls.

ATTITUDES OF SUCCESSFUL ENTREPRENEURS

While luck is definitely an attribute to success, we believe you can improve your chances of making an impact with your idea by embodying these 7 attitudes. To draw up this list, we met amazing entrepreneurs, observed and studied some of the most renowned ones such as Steve Jobs, Elon Musk, Jack Ma, Marc Benioff and many more. If you apply them, these attitudes may help you to increase your chances of success. To get you in the spirit, I also selected powerful quotes to illustrate each of these attitudes.

THE ATTITUDES OF SUCCESSFUL ENTREPRENEURS

ATTITUDE #1 – HAVE A SENSE OF PURPOSE, BE PASSIONATE!

Think big and beyond money. Everyone wants to be rich but to become rich you need to think differently. Don't think like everyone. Think about creating value, bringing a solution that changes the game and improves people's lives. Work on something you love, that matters to you.

"If you just work on stuff that you like and you're passionate about, you don't have to have a master plan with how things will play out." -
Mark Zuckerberg (Founder of Facebook)

ATTITUDE #2 – OVERCOME YOUR FEARS, TRY!

You will have hundreds of fears before you start, succeed and ultimately reach success. Entrepreneurship can be scary for a first timer. What if I fail? What if customers don't like the product? What will people say? Fear is one of the top reasons for people not doing what they want to do or what they believe in their hearts. Fear is a creativity killer. True entrepreneurs have fears but they take it upon themselves to overcome them. The way to do that is to accept the idea of failure. Failing is not the end of the world and it is a time when you learn the most. Often an entrepreneur must fail several times before he or she reaches the level of understanding that helps him or her succeed. People who never fail are people who stay in their comfort zone and do not move forward or make progress.

"Remembering that you are going to die is the best way I know of avoiding the trap of thinking you have something to lose" Steve Jobs (Founder of Apple)

ATTITUDE #3 – WORK HARD, HARDER THAN EVERYONE ELSE!

Entrepreneurship is very hard. Start-up entrepreneurs can be working day, nights, weekends. Don't underestimate it, it is not a get rich quick scheme. Launching a start-up is tough and only hard workers survive.

"Being an entrepreneur is like eating glass and staring into the abyss. If you feel like you are up for that then start a company" Elon Musk (Founder Tesla, SpaceX)

ATTITUDE #4 – NETWORK, BUILD TRUSTING RELATIONSHIPS!

In the end, it's all about people. People create opportunities. You need to network all the time, building relationships based on trust. The best way to do this is to give before you ask. Entrepreneurs are very helpful towards each other: it's the "You do me a favor, I do you a favor" mentality. In addition, when everyone has that mindset, it is healthy for the whole start-up eco-system because it is easier to make progress on your projects than in a place where everyone ignores you or slams doors on you. In the United States, land of opportunities, especially in California Silicon Valley, the networking is extremely dynamic and it is relatively easy to connect with people and get support, mentoring, help or introductions to someone else. Just say "Yes" when someone asks you a favor, this will give you not only a good karma but also emotional credit for you to ask a favor back: This is one of the secrets of networking and building trust.

"Above all, find people who inspire you and who you can learn from, then work like crazy to not let them (or yourself!) down" Clara Shih (CEO and founder of Hearsay labs and author of the Facebook era)

ATTITUDE #5 – FOCUS ON EXECUTION, MOVE FAST!!

This is simple, increase the doing time, reduce the planning time: Increase the time spent in front of your customers, venture capitalists, partners, suppliers and reduce the time in front of your computer or business plan. Not executing is one of the reasons for failure. Set clear goals and stay focused on meeting these goals: Don't procrastinate! Do everything with a sense of urgency because it takes a lot of time to be successful, sometimes even a lot of mistakes before you get it right.

"The way to get started is to quit talking and start doing" Walt Disney (Founder of Walt Disney)

ATTITUDE #6 – PERSIST AND PIVOT (CHANGE) IF NEEDED

Things are more than likely not going to go as planned or as you want. You will have very high moments and very low moments. Don't give up! You need to persist and believe that things are going to come together. Keep an open mind also. If you fail, learn and adjust your idea. Adapt fast! You might have a product/ service in mind, but after testing it you may realize that improvements and even that a complete change of direction is needed. Just don't give up. Entrepreneurship is not easy and can be a lonely adventure in some cases, especially when you start. Knowing this in advance can help, but what matters most is to keep on trying again and again until it works.

"There is a difference between failing and failure. Failing is trying something that you learn doesn't work. Failure is throwing in the towel and giving up" Jay Samit (Serial entrepreneur, CEO and author of book Disrupt You)

ATTITUDE #7 – WORK HARD, BUT DON'T FORGET TO LIVE. ENJOY EVERY STAGE OF THE JOURNEY

Work, live, love, laugh, go to the gym, eat healthy, appreciate nature or do whatever it takes for you to stay happy and positive. Being balanced will help you keep that well-needed optimism that will help you move forward and believe in your path.

"I don't think of work as work and play as play. It's all living." Sir Richard Branson

START-UPS, INNOVATION FRIENDLY ENVIRONMENTS AND KEY PLAYERS

This section focuses on defining the environment that fosters innovation. While the perfect environment may seem unimportant to most entrepreneurs seeking to start their own venture, there is much to gain from the right setting. Silicon Valley has some characteristics that foster both innovation and completion, hence the fast growth of many start-ups.

Silicon Valley has created the perfect eco-system for start-ups. As a result, new companies spurt from the ground like buds, creating jobs, economic sustainability, and growth. Regions like the Silicon Valley that implement start-up friendly eco-systems understand the economic benefits: increasing the overall competitive landscape of a region, renewing products portfolio, and more.

Keep in mind that not all eco-systems are created equal. Some, due to their size, are even difficult to find and infiltrate.

The table below outlines the various players and the roles they play in creating the perfect eco-systems for innovation that you can find in the Silicon Valley and many other regions of the world. More and more eco-systems like this are being put in place as we have entered the era of endless innovation.

Universities
<ul><li>Conduct research and develop new ideas and products with their students.</li><li>Protect intellectual property that they can either license, sell, or in rare cases waived to others.</li><li>Train students in business and technical aspects (train engineers, scientists, etc.)</li><li>Serve as bridges between students, faculty members, industry experts, investors and their students.</li><li>In some cases, provide incubator or makers' space for their community members (examples: Harvard I Lab, MIT Entrepreneurship, Stanford University etc.)</li></ul>
Incubators
<ul><li>Connect all stakeholders.</li></ul>

- Organize events to mix the different players and "teach" the start-up process
- Create opportunities for entrepreneurs to pitch their ideas to obtain funding.
- May require a stake in the company or a fee in exchange for their services

Plug n' Plays

- Share the same characteristics as incubators, generally
- Provide in addition, office space, mail box, meeting rooms to entrepreneurs
- Identify top businesses within their community and give them the opportunity to meet investors (or corporations)
- May request a fee and stake in company
- Pair corporations with innovators to facilitate acquisition or partnerships

Investors

- Business angels: individuals with more than comfortable financial means (accredited by the Stock Exchange commission).
- Venture capitalists: specialized firms that invest in start-ups and generally add significant value
- Constantly seek new opportunities for investment (what is called deal flow in the start-up world).
- The preferred goal is usually to make a return of 10X plus.

Crowdfunding sites
• These sites (for example: Indigo, GoFundMe, Kickstarter) allow potential customers to fund ideas for a reward (e.g. the product at cost etc.) • Sites like Dragon Innovation go beyond the sole aspect of funding but also get involved in the process aspect (manufacturing etc.). Dragon Innovation helps recently funded start-ups to manufacture their products.
Media
• Media, local newspapers, TV news, online specialized websites and blogs. • They relay the information, share the stories, inspire readers and viewers. • They help create and maintain the culture in the region. • Media play a very important role as they are the drum beat that keeps the eco-system moving.
Established Companies
• Big companies are sources of inspiration for aspiring entrepreneurs • They innovate augmenting the competitive landscape • Established companies sometimes struggle to keep the pace of innovation and prefer proceeding to acquisitions of new technology. This is a major incentive for entrepreneurs as it can be their hope to sell their company to a corporation.

- In addition, said companies can provide great partnership opportunities to start-ups. For example, selling the product of a start-up exclusively through their major distribution channels.

Celebrities and Influencers

- There is a growing trend of using celebrity sponsors to promote new technology. This trend grew as the entertainment industry was facing revenue losses due to the digitalization of music (streaming, free downloading sites, streaming etc.)
- Celebrities and influencers in social media are the perfect ambassadors for a particular sector of the market, in exchange for equity, royalties or commissions etc.
- *Cool Story:* Beats by Dre
  - o The company markets new headphones paired with a unique design to create the ultimate listening experience. Dr. Dre's partnership with the founders gave them the opportunity to get his million fans to test and sell the product. The Beats by Dre was an instant hit. Ultimately, the company was noticed by Apple and was acquired for a billion dollars. Entrepreneurs (and artists) should keep their ideas open to opportunities such as this one and create win-win situations between the parties involved.

Other entrepreneurs
<ul><li>Other entrepreneurs are your peers more than your competition</li><li>It is key to network with other entrepreneurs like you:<ul><li>They can be a source of great learnings and inspiration by sharing their successes or failures</li><li>They have contacts you may need and you may be able to help them with your contacts</li><li>They might be your future team of "superstars" for your start-up</li><li>They could bring to you new opportunities and help you with your business idea</li></ul></li></ul>

The Silicon Valley Plus: When business meets Tolerance and Peace!

- The culture of entrepreneurship: Diversity in entrepreneurship is a strength. No matter what ethnicity or background you are, what matters, in this land of opportunity, is what you bring to the table. The idea is that by mixing people from different backgrounds, origins and countries, you will create brainstorming sessions that have more chance to deliver unique outputs and solutions designed for global markets. By not bringing new people to the table, you will not change the inputs and therefore it is more difficult to change the outputs. Immigration should be embraced and seen as a chance. Too many countries (or companies) still do not appreciate this and consequently miss these opportunities. We believe that innovation can be a way to unify people under a common goal, a goal that is generally good for the economy, and we know that with a healthy economy come fewer problems.

In this section, you will learn how to launch your idea by preparing yourself with the necessary documentation and understanding so you can start reaching out to your first customers, investors, future team or partners.

The topics we will cover in this section are:

- The different types of business ideas you can come up with.
- How to model your idea, define who your customers are using a tool called a business model canvas.
- How to conduct a market research if you have never done so before.
- How to document your business idea using the standard documents for start-up (Pitch Presentation, Executive Summary).

WHAT IS YOUR BUSINESS IDEA?

Below are the 4 major business ideas you may find, with a description for each. As you will notice from the definitions provided, we define a business idea not just solely by its product or technology, but by the full "solution" offered. This includes the product and its features, the business model, processes and brand. <u>Innovation does not limit itself to just the product</u>: This is important to remember.

- **The Breakthrough Idea:** You are the only player or one of the very few currently developing the solution you are thinking about. This would be a great situation, although we want to warn you that this is not a common situation. With billions of people on the planet, it is statistically improbable that you are the only one to have the idea. You should compete and work at making the product or business model better and unique (differentiating it from the others). Competition in business is normal- it is all about adding (unfair) advantages and speed to the market. People who come up with breakthrough ideas are generally experts in the field and understand well the market, or are just very lucky. One issue with breakthrough ideas is that it can take a lot of time (and money) to educate the customer about why he should adopt the new breakthrough solution.

- **Re-applied or Emulated Idea:** There are players in the market but they only play in a specific application, one city, country or region of the world. You can then decide to develop and implement the same idea in another application, or untapped promising market, by adapting the solution to the market's culture or language. Many "Emulated" ideas can be very successful.

Think about Amazon.com and Alibaba.com or LinkedIn and other online professional networks like Viadeo (a platform like LinkedIn). Some emulated ideas are acquired by the players in place who want to expand their reach. Emulating an idea includes some complexity nevertheless, primarily with regards to intellectual property.

- **Ameliorated Idea:** There are other players, but the ameliorated idea has improved features such as better product specifications, existing pain points are fixed, a better business model, and added services or a differentiating brand.

- **Acquired idea:** You decide that instead of developing your new idea you would rather acquire someone else's idea to run the business. You could for example decide to buy the intellectual property from someone or a university or simply buy a start-up. The acquisition process and due diligence is complex. We will not be covering this in detail in this e-book. This is something corporations do often, called external innovation through acquisition.

Note on competition: There will always be competition and not being the only player is not necessary a problem, in fact it can even be a good thing in the case of very innovative products. Sometimes having other players on the market allows for a bigger and faster market adoption for the new product, as your competitors will also promote their product (through advertising etc.) which may help create more market reach and demand for the new technology.

Design your business model using a "Canvas"

This part will explain how to use what we believe is a very powerful tool to design and clarify your business model. The Business Model Canvas is great because it is a relatively simple tool to use to quickly provide architecture to your full solution. Later it can be used to communicate it to others. All this on just one page!

Let's see how to complete a business model canvas. Note: Do your best and forget the rest! It will take several attempts before you master this tool.

Business Model Canvass: see next page

Strategic Partners	Activities	Value Proposition	Customer relationships	Customers
Include here your strategic partners	Describe the main activities you will be performing to run the business	Describe the value proposition for your customers. i.e. What benefits they will receive out of the solution you propose compared to other comparable solutions.	How will you manage customers relationship	Describe and categorize the customers you are targeting.
	Resources / Advantages Describe your main advantages and resources		**Growth drivers** How will you grow fast?	Be as precise as possible (Location, age, ethnicity, economic class, situation, primary, secondary customers etc.)
		Competition		
		Established List your top 5 well established competitors	**New comers** List your top 5 competitors that are new entrants / start-ups	**Sales Channels** By what means you will sell your products?
Technology Describe the key technologies that will support your solution				
Cost Structure Break down the cost structure in big buckets and sort from top cost to lowest cost			**Revenue Streams** Break down the revenue streams (i.e. how you will be making money) in big buckets and sort from highest revenue generating stream to lowest	

Story: **The Silicon Napkin**: In the early years of the entrepreneurship boom, it is said that entrepreneurs would define their business model on a simple napkin, later coined the "Silicon Valley Napkin". This was just before the infamous "dot com" bubble burst. Entrepreneurs would use these sometimes poorly thought through business models to pitch to investors and would be successful at gaining funding. Obviously, this did not always work out and times have changed. Investors have learned and today require far more than just a napkin before providing funds to help you launch your business. In the rest of this e-book we will provide you with some of these requirements and the steps you will need to take to increase your chances of getting funded.

CONDUCT YOUR MARKET RESEARCH

Market research is a key step in validating and refining your business idea. It aims to provide you with a better understanding of the competition and landscape. We have put together the 6 steps below to help you to conduct your market research.

Table: The 6 steps to help you do a market research:

Step 1: Identify key stakeholders	Step 2: Research stakeholder information	Step 3: Review financial information and investor communication when available
List the key players for your idea on a piece of paper or white board. - Your competitors - The industry leaders - Any potential customers - Any potential partners - Any potential suppliers for your technology - Industry associations and clubs related to your idea - Top universities in the field for your idea - Laws that regulate the market for your idea	Search for the organizations' names and/or the key stakeholders you have identified: - Browse their websites - Find out their latest news and releases - Identify the products that compete with yours - Research the available patents database - Take notes of key individuals that are mentioned (i.e. CEOs, founders, law makers etc.) In general, by doing this step you will identify new key stakeholders. Add them to the list under step 1 and do step 2 for them also. It is an iterative process.	If your key stakeholders are listed on the stock exchange they have to report on financial and sometimes high level strategic information. In addition, they sometimes need to explain market trends, etc. to their investors This is easy information to find. It generally appears on the investor section of listed companies. Look for: - Latest annual reports - Presentations they have made to investors or at investment conferences - Any communication about their strategy - Identify those who are actively seeking to acquire new companies or technologies. - Takes notes on key individuals that are mentioned (investor relations contacts, business development managers, etc.)

Step 4:	Step 5:	Step 6:
Attend industry events and network	**Other ways to get information**	**Summarize your learning**
Trade shows can be a really good way to get a quick overview of the different players and be able to touch and feel products, brands etc. You will also have the opportunity to network with industry peers, suppliers and customers. Look out for trade shows for your ideas market. Note: these can be costly. Less expensive, yet effective are Meet-up groups or events. Check out meetup.com or Eventbrite.com, for example.	There are other ways to complete your research, such as: - Purchasing on line standard reports - Purchasing a custom report (tailored to your needs) - Subscribing to magazines and newspapers or online blogs for your field - Reading books on the field - Customer surveys or interviews - Connecting with the industry professionals in your field. They are usually connected and know the market.	Once you have completed some or all of the steps, you can finalize the process by summarizing your learning. Document in a presentation or word document what you found out with regards to (for example): - Opportunities for the market - Challenges in the market - Outlook and reasons - Mergers and acquisitions dynamics - Technology evolution, trends and specifications - Political factors and law changes that could or will affect the market - Some numbers: market size, growth, etc. - Who are the leaders, new entrants etc. At that point you should have a good market understanding.

IMPORTANT: Remember to try spending more time doing than planning. It is with your customers that you will learn the most. Try to get face-to-face time with them as soon as possible, even if you just have your idea and you do not yet have your product. Limit the amount of time you will spend doing the market research. We recommend you block yourself one day or 2 full days at the most to conduct steps 1-3. Then complete 3-6 as you go and continuously update yourself. Stay tuned to the market dynamics and changes.

COMPLETING A PITCH PRESENTATION AND EXECUTIVE SUMMARY

The Pitch Presentation and Executive Summary are critical tools to be able to communicate your idea as you start networking. As you will see in the next section, networking and engaging with as many people as you can will help you get your idea started faster. Test it with your friends, family and, better still, with your first customers. Find your team and potential investors.

The Pitch Presentation and Executive Summary document contains a limited number of slides to help you present your idea in a clear and concise manner, covering the key elements.

THE TRADITIONAL PITCH PRESENTATION SLIDES:

Below is a guideline to help you build a pitch presentation of about 9 Slides. While you may add as many slides as needed, we recommend staying within a 10-15-slides range maximum: Less is more! You will use this presentation anytime you want to communicate your idea effectively.

Important: We recommend that you also work on the designs of your slides (logos, graphics, colors etc.). Remember that you want to make an impact with your slides and show that your business idea will become a major enterprise. The content of your slide and format will help communicate your message to people. Investing in your idea is investing in yourself!

Table: Steps to create your pitch

Slide 1 The "Purpose/story" slide	Slide 2 The "Opportunities" slide	Slide 3 The "Problem being solved" slide
Choose a professional design for your presentation. - Use this first slide to tell your story! Story telling is key to connect with others: Future partners and customers!	Describe the opportunities you are going after and explain why do it now! - Target customer facts (how many, who are they, what are their characteristics) - Market size (what is the dollar value of the market) - Market outlook (what are the trends)	Explain in simple terms the problem your idea is solving Try to use the terminologies below: - Customer needs.... - Customer wants... - Customer loves... The goal of this slide is to clarify what is the purpose for the idea
Slide 4 The "Solution(s)" slide	**Slide 5** The "Market Data & Traction" slide	**Slide 6** The" Executive Team" slide
In this slide, describe your business model, products and services - The value proposition - High level specifications - How you will deliver the value to the customer	Provide in this slide some details about your competition and how you plan to compete. - Your main competitors - Highlight any competitors you may be disrupting - How your will compete and win (price, features, other) - How many orders or potential customers do you have	This slide will provide details about who your executive team is: - List names, roles and highlight meaningful experiences that will demonstrate an ability to execute plans. - If jobs are not filled yet, provide status, plan, timeline and what you need to achieve them, e.g. funding etc.
Slide 7 The "Budget" slide	**Slide 8** The "Execution Plan" slide	**Slide 9** Your Pitch or "Million dollar" slide
In this slide provide a 1-3-year financial outlook: - Expenses you need to develop your product and/or run the business - Your expected revenue - Your expected profits and breakeven time (i.e. when you are planning to be profitable)	In this slide simply show your plan: - Break down your plan into key milestones - List the steps for each milestone. It's good to show steps you have already completed (provides assurance - you have already executed some steps) - You can add the cost of each phase as an overlay	This is the final and most important slide. We call it the Million-dollar slide. It should include: - A recap - Your ultimate pitch (what you need from your audience) - And an invitation to questions from your audience

Executive Summary

The executive summary is a sub-set to the Pitch presentation. It basically summarizes what you have in your Pitch presentation into a one-page document. See it as the "resume" for your business idea.

Name & Logo	
Pitch	
Problem(s) we are solving	*Why it's a great idea: Opportunity & Outlook*
Our Solution(s)	*Our Plan - Key Milestones*
Our Competition & how we compare	*Our Executing Team*
Funds needed	*Revenue & Profit expectations*
Accomplishments to date	*What we are looking for or need*

First Name - Last Name: Phone: Email: Address Website:	Social Networks:

The 60-seconds Pitch Presentation:

Your pitch should only take 60 seconds to convey. The idea here is that, unless you can express your plan in 60 seconds, it is neither well formulated nor easily understood. In other words, speed is an important factor when attempting to retain investors' attention. Investors see many ideas every day and to give you most chance of success, being able to communicate effectively and rapidly will be key. Here are a few tips on how to achieve this:

- Keep your presentation to 3-4 slides (including cover)
- One slide for the problem you are trying to solve and the opportunity
- One slide to present your solution and the current traction you have received
- One final slide with what you need from your audience, i.e. investment, team members etc.
- We recommend you put your logo and web address on each slide so that people in the audience have time to note down the information to contact you later
- You may have 30 to 60 seconds questions and answers from the audience. Stay calm; hopefully you know your topic. If not, you will be able to gauge it eventually. Remember: "You don't need to be great to get started, you need to get started to get great" Les Brown (motivational speaker)

The outreach phase is a critical one and you should start it as soon as possible. The results of this step will help to improve your pitch presentation, as well as your idea overall. Remember: creating a startup that has impact is an iterative process. Reaching out to potential customers early only adds to the process.

- **Networking** is key and you must start building and managing relations to be successful, i.e. your first customers, potential investors, your future team, suppliers, partners etc. We will provide an overview of the steps needed to build an online presence and how to go about networking using the new tools available.

Disclosure: in this book, we will provide you with the basics for effective networking. Should you wish to learn more on the topic visit our site. Here we have listed for you some amazing books and resources to excel on this crucial topic for entrepreneurs. Remember the quote: "Your network is your net worth" (Unknown).

- **Test your market traction**: As you share your idea with others, you receive invaluable feedback that will help test your idea and, in return, improve it.
  - o You can start with close friends and family but it is key that you test your idea with potential customers and here you will learn how to go about it as well.

CREATE YOUR ONLINE PRESENCE

Today, effective networking is equivalent to effective marketing, mostly done through social media. Learn to master the social media tools available to you to build your online presence to success.

Be seen online: Write articles, comment on posts, ask questions, participate in webinars, follow, like connect with all that you possible can!

Here is what you will need to build your online presence:

- Find a domain and custom email* (examples: www.yourstartupname.com and John.doe@yourstartupname.com)
    o collaborative tools (calendar, video conferences, shared spaces etc.)
- Create a website that has a responsive design and social network friendliness
- Ensure Search Engine Optimization (SEO)
- Create your social network profiles to start building a network
- Equip yourself with tools to help you to network while managing your brand:
    o Contact/Customer Relationship Management (CRM) tool
    o Tools to manage your social networks

NETWORKING

Networking is about *connecting* with people. By connecting we mean much more than simply a virtual connection on a social network. Many people have several hundred contacts, but this does not mean they have contacts they can rely on when needed, because they have not created a meaningful connection. The basis of any relationship is trust, which includes a very important emotional aspect.

Give and you shall receive:

One great way to build strong relationships is to give before you ask. As we mentioned in the 7 attitudes of entrepreneurs, networking sometimes requires simply helping others first. The point is that you never know in advance who you will need a favor from, so it is best to get into the habit of helping others. Firstly, helping others is very positive, and if you believe in karma, you will be growing this one. Secondly, the day you need help you will have more chances of asking a favor of someone from you network that you have helped before. You could ask them for their help, or introduce you to someone they know etc.

Show genuine interest:

As an entrepreneur, there is a high chance that you are very ambitious and driven. While these are great traits for an entrepreneur, they can prove to be detrimental to your networking efforts. For example, if you approach people only when you need something from them, or to sell them your product etc. they may see you as self-orientated and they may think that you are only interested in what they have, as opposed to who they are. Treat your network as a high maintenance plant. It takes a lot of time and watering before it bears fruit. In sum, build trust with your contacts and connect with them on a personal level, be patient and disciplined and regularly take care of people in your network.

- Engage in personal discussion, choose topics, have dinner, not only to talk about work or business
- Follow up with your contacts often
- Listen more than you talk. Be genuinely interested in what they have to say

Bottom line: connect with your heart, not just via your social network profile or business card. Networking is simply about making friends.

Start with simple conversations:

Don't wait until you have formal face-to-face interactions with your stakeholders to speak to them. Engage in light conversation, regularly update them on your progress, and seek feedback. This will help you gauge whether you are ready for a more formal discussion or presentation (i.e. investor pitch), or if more work needs to be done. It will also help build trust along the way and it gives you more opportunities to connect with the individuals (be aware of everyone's time though).

The top ways to "connect" with new people:

- Organize or attend events and group reunions

- Use your existing contacts who can introduce you (hence the importance of building sincere relationships based on trust)
- Use online networking (social networks), connect with new people and engage in discussions or groups
- Via your website or blog newsletter interact with the readers, newsletter subscribers or followers.

All this is great but it is a lot of work. How can I be more efficient and effective?

Yes! Networking takes a lot of time and effort but is very critical to one's success. Like the saying goes: "It's not what you know, it's who you know and who knows you!"

It is difficult to keep up personal connections, especially when you have a large network. The good news is that there are ways to manage your network more efficiently and effectively: there are some tricks and more robust tools. Some people will fully use their phone address book and take notes about the discussions they had. They may also set reminders to contact the person again and will use the notes to recall what was discussed. Others will use Excel files. You can also use tools designed for Customer Relationship Management, also known as CRMs. These have all the features you need to focus on relationships and less on the administration of your network. We recommend you use a CRM (Prosperworks is a good one we recommend). It is a relatively minor investment but if used well, it will deliver astonishing results and help you achieve your networking goals to build solid and meaningful relationships. In addition, as you expand, you will be able to use the same tool to manage your customer base.

TEST YOUR MARKET TRACTION

Your idea is just on paper, full of untested assumptions and plans, until the day you reach out to your first customers. It is critical that you begin selling your solution to customers as soon as possible, even if your product is not yet developed. Testing the market traction is important for several reasons, as follows:

- **It will show whether your solution is as great as you imagined it:** Many entrepreneurs are optimists, but putting the idea in front of customers provides a reality check that often shows that more work is needed.

- **Customers will help to improve the design of the product or the business model**: Interacting with customers gives you new ideas and requirements. It makes you understand better what matters the most to them for the product. Learning from your customers is the best way to tailor your solution and, later on, your advertisement campaigns. This will "speak" to them more and respond better to their needs.

- **If you can prove market traction** (show how many followers, video views, orders or pre-orders, e-mails in the "stay informed" newsletter, subscriptions etc.), you have a greater chance of being taken seriously by potential investors, teams, partners etc. We will talk about crowdfunding more in the Fund section but this way of funding is also a great way to prove the market traction. The idea is that you will be able to say that you managed to engage a crowd to give you the funds to elaborate a prototype, for example in exchange for a reward (such as your product at cost). This means the "market" had some interest in the product, otherwise you would not have won the campaign. You can use the funding campaign to seek additional funds.

Note: It takes some courage to go out and meet your first customers. You might come up with many excuses, such as the product is not ready, the idea is not clear, they will not like the product. Our advice is: JUST DO IT! What you will gain is experience, both good and bad. This is more valuable than anything else you can do at this stage. Be fearless, shameless, and go meet your customers!

Examples of ways to engage your first customers

- **One on one:**
At the start, try lining up some one-on-one conversations with potential customers, even friends and family.

- **Group and demo presentations:**
You can organize an event at which you will present your product. This can be either online (webinar) or face-to-face (meet-up).

Important: Beware of bias - if you engage friends and family they might be inclined to try to motivate you so find people you don't know (a "cold" network), using the networking tools we provided earlier.

Examples of questions you may want to ask at a customer demo:

- How likely are you to buy the product when it comes out?

- How likely are you to recommend the product to a friend?

- What did you like the most about the product?

- What did you like the least about the product?

- Do you have any recommendations that would improve the product?

- How much would you spend on this product?

- On a 5 stars rating how convinced are you that this product could be a hit?

- Do you have any other comments, suggestions or concerns you would like to share?

This section will cover the funding process.

- An overview of options for financing your venture

- A description of the key steps of the crowdfunding process

- Detailed view of the process to obtain funding from accredited investors

Important: Always remember that your cheapest way of funding your business is through revenue. You should try to get revenue in, before you decide about other funding options. With revenue, you don't have to give away any equity, pay any interest, or reimburse anyone. Another alternative is to self-fund your idea either by injecting your own money or time into your project. Prefer the first option though: If you cannot sell your idea before it exists, there is a high chance you will not be able to sell it when it exist.

FINANCING CHOICES

See table on next page: **Financing Options Breakdown**

way to test

elop a prototype or

ampaign. See next page.

flyers etc.)

Financing options	Crowdfunding (e.g. Indiegogo, Kickstarter)	Accredited Investors (Business Angels &Venture Capitalists meeting the SEC requirements)
Equity Based: Shares of the company are granted to investors in exchange for funds, investors will be entitled to a dividend (preferred stock) or not (common stock). Preferred stock also entitles the investor to claim assets of the company in case of bankruptcy	**YES.** Starting in 2016, Visit www.sec.gov for more information	**YES.**
Debt Based: Bonds are given to investors in exchange for funds. Bonds are similar to loans but the company only has to pay back the lenders at the end of the bond period. Interest will be paid out periodically and can be high depending on the amount of risk associated with the business. Bonds are preferred generally at more mature stages of the business.	**YES, good practice for seed funding and helps validate your market traction and get the next rounds of funding**	**YES,** but less common and not recommended
Reward Based: A reward is provided to "funders" in exchange for their contributions. Start-ups and creatives (artists etc.) use this method to finance the first stages of their project and to test their market traction.		
: A good karma is provided in ...ted funds. Typically used by ...ization to finance good cause ...ct start-ups	**YES,** but used for not for profit	Via crowdfunding only

---

Step 1
Launch the campaign

- Define your strategy and the reward you will offer:
  o We recommend you offer as a reward your product or rewards that are related to it. (i.e.: don't offer knives and forks if your product is a drone for example)
- Identify the most relevant crowdfunding site
- Get familiar with the site's terms and conditions and utilization
- Create your campaign on the site

Step 2
Promote the campaign

- Lead promotional campaigns:
  o Use your immediate network (friends, family and whom they know). Have them share the campaign
  o Use social networks (create cool videos to create the buzz)
  o Ask for endorsement (partners with internet influence to help publicize your campaign: An artist or "celebrity" blo...
  o Pay for advertisements (paid s... network ads)
  o Send frequent emails... status updates to the... engaged and excite...

Step 3
Finalize the campaign

- Finalize the le...
  o Note the le...
  o Celeb...
  o D...

This section will cover the funding process.

- An overview of options for financing your venture

- A description of the key steps of the crowdfunding process

- Detailed view of the process to obtain funding from accredited investors

Important: Always remember that your cheapest way of funding your business is through revenue. You should try to get revenue in, before you decide about other funding options. With revenue, you don't have to give away any equity, pay any interest, or reimburse anyone. Another alternative is to self-fund your idea either by injecting your own money or time into your project. Prefer the first option though: If you cannot sell your idea before it exists, there is a high chance you will not be able to sell it when it exist.

FINANCING CHOICES

See table on next page: **Financing Options Breakdown**

Financing options	Crowdfunding (e.g. Indiegogo, Kickstarter)	Accredited Investors (Business Angels &Venture Capitalists meeting the SEC requirements)
Equity Based: Shares of the company are granted to investors in exchange for funds, investors will be entitled to a dividend (preferred stock) or not (common stock). Preferred stock also entitles the investor to claim assets of the company in case of bankruptcy	**YES.** Starting in 2016, Visit www.sec.gov for more information	**YES.**
Debt Based: Bonds are given to investors in exchange for. Bonds are similar to loans but the company only has to pay back the lenders at the end of the bond period. Interest will be paid out periodically and can be high depending on the amount of risk associated with the business. Bonds are preferred generally at more mature stages of the business.		**YES,** but less common and not recommended
Reward Based: A reward is provided to "funders" in exchange for their contributions. Start-ups and creatives (artists etc.) use this method to finance the first stages of their project and to test their market traction.	**YES,** good practice for seed funding and helps validate your market traction and get the next rounds of funding	Via crowdfunding only
Donation Based: A good karma is provided in exchange for donated funds. Typically used by not for profit organization to finance good cause activities or social impact start-ups	**YES,** but used for not for profit	

CROWDFUNDING IN A NUTSHELL

The table below provides key steps of any crowdfunding campaign. More information is available from crowdfunding sites. These sites provide you with a walk through on how to navigate the site.

We encourage crowdfunding campaigns as they are a good way to test market traction and get the first funds needed to develop a prototype or product etc.

Follow these three steps to fund your campaign. See next page.

Step 1 Launch the campaign	Step 2 Promote the campaign	Step 3 Finalize the campaign & deliver the rewards
- Define your strategy and the reward you will offer: o We recommend you offer as a reward your product or rewards that are related to it. (i.e. don't offer knives and forks if your product is a drone for example) - Identify the most relevant crowdfunding site - Get familiar with the site's terms and conditions and utilization - Create your campaign on the site	- Lead promotional campaigns: o Use your immediate network (friends, family and whom they know). Have them share the campaign o Use social networks (create cool videos to create the buzz) o Ask for endorsement (partners with internet influence to help publicize your campaign: An artist or "celebrity" blogger) o Pay for advertisements (paid social network ads) o Send frequent emails, newsletters and status updates to the funders. Keep everyone engaged and excited. Be positive. o Events and street actions (distribution of flyers etc.)	- Finalize the campaign: o Note the lessons learned o Celebrate the hard work and success o Deliver the rewards as per the terms and conditions o Document the story board of the campaign and share the success stories with others (potential investors, future teams etc.) o Use the funds

Get Funded by "Accredited Investors"

Investors Criteria (SEC Rule)

Start-up investing holds a lot of risk and therefore is highly regulated by the SEC to protect those with lower financial power. As of October 2015, to be accredited, investors need to meet requirements as defined by the Securities Exchange Commission (SEC) (source: www.sec.gov):

- Income over $200,000, or $300,000 with spouse
- Income earned in the previous 2 years
- Expectation to earn same or above in the current year

Or

- Net worth of more than $1,000,000 alone or with Spouse (excluding the main home)

Or

- An organization (trust or business) with assets >$5,000,000
- Directed by "sophisticated" individual(s) (experienced people, or expert)
- The organization must not be founded solely for the targeted investment (it should be an established organization)

Or

- Any entity in which the equity is owned by accredited investors (i.e. Venture Capital firms)

Note: As of November 2015, the SEC has created a new rule to become effective in 2016 for non-accredited investors to be able to invest in start-up via the crowdfunding platform. This new rule includes very strict requirements, such as the limit on total investment, based on the income of the investor etc. Visit www.sec.gov for more information.

KEY STEPS & TIPS

In this part, we provide you with the key steps to obtain funding from accredited investors.

UNDERSTANDING WHAT INVESTORS USUALLY LOOK FOR.

Investing in a start-up is very risky. Investors know this and are willing to take calculated risks. Here are some of the elements that will reassure them:

- **Present a well- formulated idea:** Know the ins and outs of making your business work. Do your homework and be ready to back your claims when necessary.
- **Document your idea:** You have put some time in preparing your documents and made sure they are easy to navigate and comprehend.
- **Prove market traction:** You have proof that customers want or need the product (feedback, surveys, pre-orders, orders, crowdfunding campaign results etc.)
- **Showcase your talent:** You have had some experience with start-ups, good or bad, you have learned and can clearly demonstrate your experience.

- **Show competence:** Execution is critical in the startup world. Prove your team's ability to execute the business model. You should have a cross-functional team.
- **Clear legal framework:** Investors like to see what they are familiar with when it comes to business set up. In the United States, they tend to prefer a Delaware state corporation.
- **Highlight the unfair advantages:** You have clear unfair advantages that make your start-up business idea very competitive and set for fast growth. (e.g. patents, celebrity endorsement, killer team, exclusive partnership, funding, major customers already locked in, exclusivity contracts etc.)
- **Prepare an exit strategy:** An example would be that you already have targeted companies that could be interested in acquiring the business or would go public.
- **You and other stakeholders have taken the risk before them:** You are investing and dedicating time and money for your idea. Others already believed in your idea and invested etc.
- **Provide accurate financial information:** The financial figures you will be providing must make sense. You are realistic in your estimates.
- **Adapt your lexicon:** You adapt your very technical vocabulary to one they can understand. Researching your audience will give you insights on their level of expertise which informs your choice of terminology. For example, if you are a scientist or engineer, keep in mind that not everyone is.

CONNECTING WITH INVESTORS

The best way for you to connect with investors is to immerse yourself in the start-up environment (see chapter 1: Incubation phase), working with local incubators and accelerators in your areas and participating in events. You can also seek the help from the contacts in your network who are connected to business angels or venture capitalists. (It is always better if someone introduces you. Investors receive many requests, so if someone they know and trust informs them that you might have a good idea, they will be more likely to hear you out).

Another option is to try contact investors directly online (on their company's website or social media), or via specialized networking sites. Note though that this may be harder as you will be one request amongst many. We recommend working with local incubators or accelerators and your network. If you have no results, do not hesitate to seek help outside your region.

PITCHING YOUR IDEA CLEARLY & CONCISELY TO THE INVESTOR(S)

Once you have face or phone time with investors, you should pitch your idea, leveraging the documents from earlier (the Pitch document, Executive Summary and Business Model Canvas)

Here are some pieces of advice to make this a good experience for everyone:

- **Know and adapt to your audience:** It is key that you engage your audience and that you deliver a message that appeals to them. Ask your audience what they know about the field of your idea, carry out some research with them first. Tell a story that captures the curiosity and attention of the crowd. Don't simply throw your slides at them. If you can, ask your audience first what they would like to see in your presentation and adapt it accordingly.

- **Be assertive, confident and persistent:** It is less important to have an answer than to provide accurate information. Be confident enough to request time to answer a specific question. In other words, when uncertain, ask for more time. If anything, this will keep the line of communication open between you and potential investors.

- **Keep cool:** Remember that this presentation is also a test of your leadership skills. A leader maintains calm even in chaos. Take the opportunity to showcase this skill by expressing your idea in a calm and collected manner. It will increase the effectiveness of your presentation.

- **Keep it short:** Half the time, twice the benefit. Cover your pitch presentation slides in 15 minutes and leave 10-15 minutes for questions. If the investor is interested to know more he will schedule more time with you. If you don't hear from an investor quickly, he is probably not interested. When the demand is hot, so are the deals. Things happen fast.

INVESTOR'S FURTHER DUE DILIGENCE

Depending on the amount requested, the investor will want to see more information before starting their own due diligence and/or releasing funds. They will want to:

- Understand and calculate the valuation of your company
- Walk through in detail your business case or market analysis
- Review your market traction proofs that you announced at pitch time
- Review your patents and business model
- Review your product prototypes
- Seek feedback from customers, if any
- Review the profiles of your team members

Important: Some investors, especially venture capitalists, have deep experience of what works and what doesn't in a start-up venture. They might require you to change elements of your plan before disbursing funds. For example, they could require a restructure of your team if they deem the current one unfit for execution.

FUNDING ROUNDS

Investors usually invest in rounds. Each round typically corresponds to a stage of the business start-up. The reason for this is to minimize the risks and ensure you can execute the plans.

Stage	Example of stage elements
Seed or Early Stage	First or early funding stage generally used to finalize the development of the product.
Round 1 or Series A	Used to set up the operations and finance the first marketing campaigns and sales teams
Round 2 or Series B	To further scale the business and help continue take market share
Round 3 or Series C	Used to open new offices in new regions or cities
Round 4 or Series D	Continuing funding until the company becomes profitable and has reached significant market share
Exit Stage	Initial public offering, acquisition by another company, sale of shares to new shareholders

LEGAL ASPECTS TO START-UP

This part is dedicated to the legal framework of your start-up. This step, after the idea verification, represents the most important part of the process. It must not be taken lightly as it may make or break your venture. We have highlighted the key steps in setting up the legal framework of your venture.

CONSULT WITH A LAWYER

Do not forget to protect your idea and yourself. The best way to ensure protection of your venture is by seeking the advice of experts in the field, notably lawyers or attorneys who specialize in emerging growth businesses (start-ups) to set up your business in an appropriate manner. Make sure you learn as much as you can from your lawyer. As a founder or CEO it is important that you understand all major legal aspects.

DELAWARE C-CORPORATION

They are many different types of legal entities you can chose from but Delaware State incorporation is frequently used for several reasons. The state provides the most favorable tax conditions for investors. Moreover, investors are familiar with the law. Generally speaking, you are not required to incorporate before you hire or decide to share equity.

STOCK PURCHASE AGREEMENTS

Stock purchase agreements represent a means of sharing equity with investors and co-founders. For co-founders you will want to include a vesting period, during which they lose all entitlement to equity if fired or if they leave prior to the end of the period. There are exceptions of course.

EMPLOYMENT AGREEMENTS

All employees should sign an employment contract. It is important to clearly state what is the new hire contract category (Contractor or employee) to avoid issues later on.

EMPLOYEE STOCK OPTIONS

You can provide employees with stock options giving them the opportunity to purchase company stock at a preferred price. This is highly recommended for start-ups. It will ensure employees have the same motivation as the founders to see the start-up grow.

NON-DISCLOSURE AGREEMENT

If employees, investors or even partners of your business have or will have access to confidential and strategic information you will want to ensure all parties sign a non-disclosure agreement.

INTELLECTUAL PROPERTY

You can and should patent, copyright or trademark your intellectual property. Patents protect your product. Copyrights protect audio, video, or written material. Trademarks protect your brand, logos or the design of your product.

CONCLUSION

This is the end of this e-book but hopefully the start of acceleration of your entrepreneurial Journey.

The basic key concepts and information that you have read about should now give you a better understanding of where to start, how to transform an idea into a more tangible and actionable launch plan and begin the process of seeking resources and help from others. Entrepreneurship can sometimes feel like a lonely journey but it is important to realize that success will be driven by the new people that will surround you, support you and your idea as you progress: investors, your team, partners, co-founders, customers, employees and other entrepreneurs or intrapreneurs. Deals and opportunities come from people so make sure that you associate with talented individuals that have the same dreams and ambition as yourself. These are people with whom you connect at a deeper level than just the business aspect of your project, that share your purpose, vision and who will help you drive your venture forward, in the fast lane! Remember to persevere, have no fear until you succeed.

Alistair Schneider

Few things before you go off and start-up!

Did you enjoy the read? Do you have questions, comments or suggestions? Would you like to partner on a second edition?

Contact: alistair@startupsinnovation.com

Help me reach out to more entrepreneurs like you...

If you feel we have helped you with this e-book we would be delighted to see you rate and give a review of the e-book on one of the book stores you used to get a copy (e.g. Amazon.com)

Please share with your friends the bookstore e-book link. This helps us a lot and is the best way for you to show us additional love (and help your friends who are also trying hard to launch their ideas) ☺ ☺ ☺

Important Copyright notice

Please refer to full copyright notice at the front of this e-book. Creating this e-book has taken a lot of time. Please do not copy, distribute or make use of it without the express consent of its author to comply with copyright regulations in place. Hope you understand.

A French British national, has been living in the United States for the last several years. While he currently resides in Boston Massachusetts, Alistair also spent some time in the Silicon Valley, California. He is originally from Strasbourg, Alsace: A city usually known for being the eurometropole, medical innovation and last but not least it's unique food and wine!

Alistair is a Business management expert in charge of leading large initiatives and problem solving projects for tech companies, leading teams, business process design, innovation across all functions of the enterprise. He also spent many years in Finance managing nine digit plus budgets, supporting Information Technology delivery. Entrepreneurial, ambitious, passionate, he is always very keen on creating connections and working with teams that spark creative thinking and new opportunities. He masters innovation and change management tools.

In 2015, he decided to author the _Start-ups Innovation Fast lane_ book that details the steps for start-ups to innovate and describes start-up eco-systems. He also launched the Start-ups and innovation project and blog: The initial goal was to create a platform for upcoming entrepreneurs, innovation officers and ecosystems leaders to learn and accelerate their innovation projects and create a bridge between start-ups, enterprises and regional leaders.

Through this venture, he was able to interview few leading experts in the same space such as Jay Samit (Serial entrepreneur, author, speaker) and several other leaders from the Silicon Valley, Boston and beyond.

Innovation to Alistair is more than a buzzword. It is a passion and the solution to bring people together, sustain and grow existing economies, create jobs and the best way to improve the world by creating tangible value for the living. He spreads the word, influences others, at work or when speaking at events. He partners with teams, entrepreneurs, innovators, disruptors and artists with the goal to make great things happen, foster creativity and accelerate innovation.

He obtained his Master degree in Business Management from the EMD Business School of Marseille in France, has a Finance degree and strives to continuously develops himself to new and latest knowledge through readings or trainings.

He also authored a thesis about how Millipore Corporation a Life Technology company scaled and doubled its size in 5 years using a disciplined, well known strategy execution approach and focusing on people.

As part of his intrapreneurship projects he successfully developed, ground up, in an extremely short amount of time, with a Software developer an Enterprise solution that was implemented and allowed better, faster and more automated controls over financial statements of a Fortune 500 company. The solution has been used for nearly 10 consecutives years and has been automating controls over a several billion dollars balance sheet.

As an entrepreneur he also founded Junglemy an e-learning platform that provides targeted knowledge to help people acquire the knowledge they need to be live more successful and balanced lives (Courses on capitalism, investment, real estate, personal finance, entrepreneurship, business, healthy living and social skills). is currently on the board of advisors of Nutranx, a novel digital money remittance (phone top ups) system between US and Haiti using the blockchain technology. He also worked on other start-up projects in the Enterprise software, customer feedback management, entertainment arena and is always seeking to implement new ideas and solving problems.

Author's Acknowledgements:

Writing this e-book has been easier than it could have been thanks to the help and support of friends and family who kindly accepted to be part of this project by either reviewing initial drafts and providing feedback, or by accepting the time that I dedicated to this project during my spare time. Thanks everyone for your cheers, support and enthusiasm in me while completing this work. What made this activity fun was all the interactions I had with you. Some of you were more involved than others and this is why I'd like to particularly mention the people below, as they played an important role that helped me take this project to the finish line and to the level of quality it is now.

My production coordinator and editor:

Yvonne Rose (Quality Press, Production Coordinator).

Key influencers I crossed path with during this adventure and who help or provided unexpected support:

Bernard Kress (Serial entrepreneur and Microsoft HoloLens executive): Thank you Bernard for sharing your Start-ups experiences, your wealth of knowledge about the Start-up ecosystem and for the kind Foreword.

Chris Kalaboukis (Founder & CEO, hellofuture: visionary innovator, inventor): Thank you Chris for the talk we had on innovation and feedback.

Dirk Ahlborn (CEO of Hyperloop Transportation Technologies and founder of Jumpstartfund.com): Thank you Dirk for providing me with the authorization to use the picture of the future fastest terrestrial mode of transportation (Hyperloop) to illustrate the "need for speed" when it comes to innovation and launching a start-up. Good luck in your amazing venture.

Ian Knowles (Venture Capitalist, Founder Spruce & Norton): Thank you Ian for sharing your perspectives on Venture Capital and entrepreneurship.

Jay Samit (CEO, Serial entrepreneur, Author "Disrupt you") for accepting to participate in the May 2016 event and for sharing some thoughts about the e-book strategy. Sincerely honored to have connected.

Kendall Minter (Entertainment Attorney, author, speaker) thank you for your insights on the entertainment industry disruption.

Other important people that helped in some shape or form:

Adela Villanueva (Global Strategist, Innovation, Digital Transformation, Start-up mentor, Intrapreneur), **Alexandre Barthel** (Marketing Director), **Alison Butler** (Intrapreneur and Technology Consultant), **Arnaud Caspar** (Marketing Director), **Brittany Perez** (Prosperworks Account Manager), **Christophe Grimont** (Executive coach), **Caroline Hirst** (Proofreader – French to English Translator), **Christophe Gerhards** (Finance, management, intrapreneur), **Dario Bellehumeur** (Financial Director, Controller), **Derek Mathieson** (Duke MBA, Business & Strategy), **Ivy Wang** (Entrepreneur – Truelifegenie.com), **Jeffrey Ellis** (Business Analyst and, Manager, MBA Boston University), **Julian Plested** (Proofreader – Self-employed), **James Grimont** (Student) **and Robert Grimont** (Business founder), **Khalid Mohammed** (Accenture Consultant), **Olivier De Souza** (Entrepreneur, Artist and manufacturing specialist) **Ridouane**

Amallah (Business Technology Sourcing Director and Marathons des Sables candidate), **Sheri Mason** (Senior Attorney - Boston), **Yue Wu** (Start-up founder Buy Time Medical Inc.), **Wyn Schneider** (Proofreader) and **Yannick Schneider** (Linguist, Life Technology Sales expert, author), Special thanks to **Nora Gay** (Founder of CGRSS and NuTranx) for your support all throughout this project. All people I worked with on various projects at **Merck Kgaa**, **MilliporeSigma**, **Cambridge Technology**, **NDS. Friends and family** for the support and love!

Thanks all